Simple Sermon Notes

For Kids Ages 7-12

By Brett & Amanda Bell

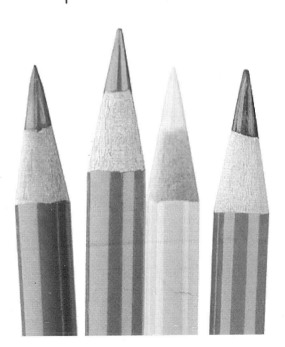

Simple Sermon Notes: For Kids Ages 7-12

ISBN: 1533427046
ISBN-13: 978-1533427045

New Life Overnight
newlifeovernight.com
Facebook - Twitter - Pinterest - Blog - Instagram

Do you ever get bored during the church service? Is the sermon hard to understand sometimes? Do you forget what church was about after you leave?

Simple Sermon Notes is here to help!

Now you can keep track of what the preacher is talking about in a fun and easy to follow workbook.

HOLDS 52 SERMONS

2 PAGES FOR EACH SERMON

Page 1

Page 2

Flip the page to get started. ➡

Sermon Title (or Subject)

_____

Date

_____

Today's Bible Verses

_____
_____
_____

Key Words

When you hear one of the words below...put a check by it.

- ☐ Grace
- ☐ God
- ☐ Bible
- ☐ Jesus
- ☐ Faith
- ☐ Glory
- ☐ Heaven
- ☐ Repent
- ☐ Crucified
- ☐ Peace
- ☐ Trial
- ☐ Mercy
- ☐ Love
- ☐ Gospel
- ☐ Saved

Notes:

Write your favorite things about today's sermon.

_____
_____
_____
_____
_____
_____
_____
_____
_____
_____
_____

Draw a Picture of Today's Bible Story

My Favorite Song From Today is...

COUNT How many times the preacher says the word "God."

~~HHH~~ I

Pray   Write Things You Want to pray for.

I Love...

Sermon Title (or Subject)

_____

Date

_____

Today's Bible Verses

_____
_____
_____

Key Words

When you hear one of the words below...put a check by it.

- [ ] Holy
- [ ] Serve
- [ ] Lord
- [ ] Cross
- [ ] Sacrifice
- [ ] Gift
- [ ] Worship
- [ ] Charity
- [ ] Spirit
- [ ] Power
- [ ] Hope
- [ ] Joy
- [ ] Give
- [ ] Blessed
- [ ] Prophet

Notes:

Write your favorite things about today's sermon.

Draw a Picture of Today's Bible Story

My Favorite Song From Today is...

Count How many times the preacher says the word "Jesus."

Pray Write Things You want to pray for.

I Love...

Sermon Title (or Subject)

_____

Date

_____

Today's Bible Verses

_____
_____
_____

Key Words

When you hear one of the words below...put a check by it.

- ☐ Altar
- ☐ Pray
- ☐ Obey
- ☐ Help
- ☐ Temple
- ☐ Christ
- ☐ Rose
- ☐ Grave
- ☐ Israel
- ☐ Baptize
- ☐ Sing
- ☐ Study
- ☐ Word
- ☐ Amen
- ☐ Scripture

Notes:

Write your favorite things about today's sermon.

_____
_____
_____
_____
_____
_____
_____
_____
_____

Draw a Picture of Today's Bible Story

My Favorite Song From Today is...

Count How many times the preacher says the word "Lord."

~~HHH~~ I

Pray   Write Things You Want to pray for.

I Love...

Sermon Title (or Subject)

_____

Date

_____

Today's Bible Verses

_____
_____
_____

Key Words

When you hear one of the words below...put a check by it.

- ☐ Apostle
- ☐ Ark
- ☐ Follow
- ☐ Birth
- ☐ Bless
- ☐ Blood
- ☐ Child
- ☐ Church
- ☐ Comfort
- ☐ Eternal
- ☐ Father
- ☐ Fruit
- ☐ Gospel
- ☐ Heart
- ☐ Life

Notes:

Write your favorite things about today's sermon.

_____
_____
_____
_____
_____
_____
_____
_____
_____
_____
_____

Draw a Picture of Today's Bible Story

My Favorite Song From Today is…

_____

_____

_____

Count How many times the preacher says the word "Spirit."

~~IIII~~ I

Pray Write Things You Want to pray for.

_____

_____

_____

_____

I Love…

Sermon Title (or Subject)

_____

Date

_____

Today's Bible Verses

_____
_____
_____

Key Words

When you hear one of the words below...put a check by it.

- ☐ Son
- ☐ Lust
- ☐ Mercy
- ☐ Grace
- ☐ Preach
- ☐ King
- ☐ Saint
- ☐ Sheep
- ☐ Thank
- ☐ Sin
- ☐ Trust
- ☐ Work
- ☐ Unity
- ☐ Study
- ☐ Victory

Notes:

Write your favorite things about today's sermon.

_____
_____
_____
_____
_____
_____
_____
_____
_____
_____
_____
_____

Draw a Picture of Today's Bible Story

My Favorite Song From Today is...

Count
How many times the preacher says the word "Bible."

HHH I

Pray Write Things You Want to pray for.

I Love...

Sermon Title (or Subject)

_____

Date

_____

Today's Bible Verses

_____
_____
_____

Key Words

When you hear one of the words below...put a check by it.

- [ ] Sea
- [ ] God
- [ ] Bible
- [ ] Mother
- [ ] Faith
- [ ] Glory
- [ ] Heaven
- [ ] Father
- [ ] Crucified
- [ ] Land
- [ ] Trial
- [ ] Jerusalem
- [ ] Love
- [ ] Gospel
- [ ] Saved

Notes:

Write your favorite things about today's sermon.

_____
_____
_____
_____
_____
_____
_____
_____
_____
_____

Draw a Picture of Today's Bible Story

My Favorite Song From Today is...

_____

_____

_____

Count How many times the preacher says the word "Family."

卌 I

Pray   Write things you want to pray for.

I Love...

Sermon Title (or Subject)

_____

Date

_____

Today's Bible Verses

_____
_____
_____

Key Words

When you hear one of the words below...put a check by it.

☐ Holy   ☐ Serve   ☐ Lord

☐ Moses   ☐ Sacrifice   ☐ Gift

☐ Worship   ☐ Charity   ☐ Testament

☐ Jewish   ☐ Hope   ☐ Joy

☐ Give   ☐ Blessed   ☐ Prophet

Notes:

Write your favorite things about today's sermon.

_____
_____
_____
_____
_____
_____
_____
_____
_____
_____
_____

Draw a Picture of Today's Bible Story

My Favorite Song From Today is...

_____

_____

_____

Count How many times the preacher says the word "Live."

~~HH~~I

Pray Write Things you want to pray for.

_____

_____

_____

_____

I Love...

Sermon Title (or Subject)

_____

Date

_____

Today's Bible Verses

_____
_____
_____

Key Words

When you hear one of the words below...put a check by it.

- ☐ Change
- ☐ Bow
- ☐ Obey
- ☐ Help
- ☐ Temple
- ☐ Christ
- ☐ Flesh
- ☐ King
- ☐ Israel
- ☐ Baptize
- ☐ Sing
- ☐ Study
- ☐ World
- ☐ Amen
- ☐ Scripture

Notes:

Write your favorite things about today's sermon.

_____
_____
_____
_____
_____
_____
_____
_____
_____
_____
_____

Draw a Picture of Today's Bible Story

My Favorite Song From Today is…

_____

_____

_____

Count

How many times the preacher says the word "New."

HHH I

Pray   Write Things You Want to pray for.

_____

_____

_____

_____

I Love…

Sermon Title (or Subject)

_____

Date

_____

Today's Bible Verses

_____
_____
_____

Key Words

When you hear one of the words below...put a check by it.

☐ Paul   ☐ Pride   ☐ Believe

☐ Saved   ☐ Bless   ☐ Blood

☐ Child   ☐ Church   ☐ Boat

☐ Know   ☐ Father   ☐ Fruit

☐ Gospel   ☐ Heart   ☐ Life

Notes:

Write your favorite things about today's sermon.

_____
_____
_____
_____
_____
_____
_____
_____
_____
_____
_____

Draw a Picture of Today's Bible Story

My Favorite Song From Today is...

Count

How many times the preacher says the word "Come."

~~HHH~~ I

Pray   Write Things You Want to pray for.

I Love...

Sermon Title (or Subject)

_____

Date

_____

Today's Bible Verses

_____
_____
_____

Key Words

When you hear one of the words below...put a check by it.

- [ ] Help
- [ ] Way
- [ ] Mercy
- [ ] Listen
- [ ] Preach
- [ ] Love
- [ ] Saint
- [ ] Sheep
- [ ] Thank
- [ ] Good
- [ ] Trust
- [ ] Work
- [ ] Walk
- [ ] Study
- [ ] Victory

Notes:

Write your favorite things about today's sermon.

_____
_____
_____
_____
_____
_____
_____
_____
_____
_____

Draw a Picture of Today's Bible Story

My Favorite Song From Today is...

Count How many times the preacher says the word "Heart."

Pray Write Things You Want to pray for.

I Love...

Sermon Title (or Subject)

_____

Date

Today's Bible Verses

_____
_____
_____

Key Words
When you hear one of the words below...put a check by it.

- ☐ Ark
- ☐ God
- ☐ Bible
- ☐ Jesus
- ☐ Son
- ☐ Scripture
- ☐ Heaven
- ☐ Fruit
- ☐ Crucified
- ☐ Peace
- ☐ Trial
- ☐ Mercy
- ☐ Love
- ☐ Trust
- ☐ Saved

Notes:
Write your favorite things about today's sermon.

_____
_____
_____
_____
_____
_____
_____
_____
_____
_____

Draw a Picture of Today's Bible Story

My Favorite Song From Today is...

Count How many times the preacher says the word "Life."

HHT I

Pray Write Things You Want to pray for.

I Love...

Sermon Title (or Subject)

_____

Date

_____

Today's Bible Verses

_____
_____
_____

Key Words

When you hear one of the words below...put a check by it.

- ☐ Amen
- ☐ Serve
- ☐ Mercy
- ☐ Cross
- ☐ Sacrifice
- ☐ Gift
- ☐ Worship
- ☐ Trust
- ☐ Spirit
- ☐ Work
- ☐ Hope
- ☐ Joy
- ☐ Give
- ☐ Blessed
- ☐ Unity

Notes:

Write your favorite things about today's sermon.

_____
_____
_____
_____
_____
_____
_____
_____
_____
_____

✏️ Draw a Picture of Today's Bible Story

My Favorite Song From Today is...

Count
How many times the preacher says the word "Amen."

॥॥ I

Pray Write Things You Want to pray for.

I Love...

Sermon Title (or Subject)

_____

Date
_____

Today's Bible Verses

_____
_____
_____

Key Words
When you hear one of the words below...put a check by it.

- ☐ Altar
- ☐ Pray
- ☐ Obey
- ☐ Word
- ☐ Sin
- ☐ Saint
- ☐ Rose
- ☐ Grave
- ☐ Israel
- ☐ Heart
- ☐ Sing
- ☐ Study
- ☐ Blood
- ☐ Amen
- ☐ Scripture

Notes:
Write your favorite things about today's sermon.

_____
_____
_____
_____
_____
_____
_____
_____
_____
_____
_____

Draw a Picture of Today's Bible Story

My Favorite
Song From
Today is...

Count
How many times
the preacher
says the word
"Sin."

||||| |

Pray   Write Things You Want to pray for.

I Love...

Sermon Title (or Subject)

_____

Date

_____

Today's Bible Verses

_____
_____
_____

Key Words

When you hear one of the words below...put a check by it.

- ☐ Grace
- ☐ Ark
- ☐ Believe
- ☐ Birth
- ☐ Lust
- ☐ Blood
- ☐ Sheep
- ☐ Church
- ☐ Preach
- ☐ Eternal
- ☐ Father
- ☐ Fruit
- ☐ Gospel
- ☐ Jesus
- ☐ Life

Notes:

Write your favorite things about today's sermon.

_____
_____
_____
_____
_____
_____
_____
_____
_____
_____
_____

Draw a Picture of Today's Bible Story

My Favorite Song From Today is...

_____

_____

_____

Count How many times the preacher says the word "Grace."

꜊꜊꜊꜊꜊ |

Pray   Write Things You Want to pray for.

_____

_____

_____

_____

I Love...

Sermon Title (or Subject)

_____

Date

_____

Today's Bible Verses

_____
_____
_____

Key Words

When you hear one of the words below...put a check by it.

- ☐ Repent
- ☐ Lust
- ☐ Mercy
- ☐ Grace
- ☐ God
- ☐ Crucify
- ☐ Saint
- ☐ Sheep
- ☐ Thank
- ☐ Sin
- ☐ Trust
- ☐ Love
- ☐ Saved
- ☐ Study
- ☐ Victory

Notes:

Write your favorite things about today's sermon.

_____
_____
_____
_____
_____
_____
_____
_____
_____
_____
_____

Draw a Picture of Today's Bible Story

My Favorite Song From Today is...

_____

_____

_____

Count how many times the preacher says the word "Cross."

Pray   Write Things You Want to pray for.

I LOVE...

Sermon Title (or Subject)

_____

Date

_____

Today's Bible Verses

_____
_____
_____

Key Words

When you hear one of the words below...put a check by it.

- ☐ Holy
- ☐ God
- ☐ Bible
- ☐ Gift
- ☐ Book
- ☐ Glory
- ☐ Heaven
- ☐ Repent
- ☐ Crucified
- ☐ Joy
- ☐ Author
- ☐ Mercy
- ☐ Love
- ☐ Gospel
- ☐ Pray

Notes:

Write your favorite things about today's sermon.

Draw a Picture of Today's Bible Story

My Favorite Song From Today is...

Count how many times the preacher says the word "Look."

$\cancel{||||}$ 1

Pray   Write Things you want to pray for.

I Love...

Sermon Title (or Subject)

_____

Date

_____

Today's Bible Verses

_____
_____
_____

Key Words

When you hear one of the words below...put a check by it.

- ☐ Spirit
- ☐ Serve
- ☐ Lord
- ☐ Cross
- ☐ Peace
- ☐ Gift
- ☐ Love
- ☐ Charity
- ☐ Page
- ☐ King
- ☐ Hope
- ☐ Joy
- ☐ Give
- ☐ Vision
- ☐ Blind

Notes:

Write your favorite things about today's sermon.

_____
_____
_____
_____
_____
_____
_____
_____
_____
_____
_____

Draw a Picture of Today's Bible Story

My Favorite Song From Today is...

Count
How many times the preacher says the word "Listen."

𝗛𝗛𝗛 𝟏

Pray
Write things you want to pray for.

I Love...

Sermon Title (or Subject)

_____

Date

_____

Today's Bible Verses

_____

Key Words

When you hear one of the words below...put a check by it.

- ☐ Lamb
- ☐ Pray
- ☐ Obey
- ☐ Help
- ☐ Thank
- ☐ Christ
- ☐ Comfort
- ☐ Grave
- ☐ Bless
- ☐ Blood
- ☐ Sing
- ☐ Garden
- ☐ Word
- ☐ Gift
- ☐ Scripture

Notes:

Write your favorite things about today's sermon.

_____
_____
_____
_____
_____
_____
_____
_____
_____
_____
_____

Draw a Picture of Today's Bible Story

My Favorite Song From Today is...

_____
_____
_____

Count
How many times the preacher says the word "Gospel."

Pray   Write Things You want to pray for.
_____
_____
_____
_____

I Love...

Sermon Title (or Subject)

_____

Date

_____

Today's Bible Verses

_____
_____
_____

Key Words

When you hear one of the words below...put a check by it.

☐ Grave   ☐ Ark   ☐ Israel

☐ Birth   ☐ Sing   ☐ Blood

☐ Study   ☐ Church   ☐ Comfort

☐ Child   ☐ Father   ☐ Virgin

☐ Gospel   ☐ Heart   ☐ Life

Notes:

Write your favorite things about today's sermon.

_____
_____
_____
_____
_____
_____
_____
_____
_____
_____
_____

Draw a Picture of Today's Bible Story

My Favorite Song From Today is...

Count
How many times the preacher says the word "Him."

HHT I

Pray   Write Things You Want to pray for.

I Love...

Sermon Title (or Subject)

_____

Date

_____

Today's Bible Verses

_____
_____
_____

Key Words
When you hear one of the words below...put a check by it.

☐ Peter   ☐ Lust   ☐ Mercy

☐ Power   ☐ Preach   ☐ King

☐ Saint   ☐ Sheep   ☐ Pure

☐ Bible   ☐ Trust   ☐ Work

☐ Follow   ☐ Study   ☐ Trust

Notes:
Write your favorite things about today's sermon.

_____
_____
_____
_____
_____
_____
_____
_____
_____
_____
_____

Draw a Picture of Today's Bible Story

My Favorite Song From Today is...

_____
_____
_____

Count
How many times the preacher says the word "Church."

~~HHT~~ I

Pray   Write Things You want to pray for.
_____
_____
_____
_____

I Love...

Sermon Title (or Subject)

_____

Date

_____

Today's Bible Verses

_____
_____
_____

Key Words

When you hear one of the words below...put a check by it.

- ☐ Prince
- ☐ Woman
- ☐ Bible
- ☐ Book
- ☐ Faith
- ☐ Glory
- ☐ Heaven
- ☐ Faith
- ☐ Crucified
- ☐ Egypt
- ☐ Trial
- ☐ Mercy
- ☐ Love
- ☐ Death
- ☐ Saved

Notes:

Write your favorite things about today's sermon.

_____
_____
_____
_____
_____
_____
_____
_____
_____
_____
_____

Draw a Picture of Today's Bible Story

My Favorite Song From Today is...

Count How many times the preacher says the word "we."

~~HHH~~ I

Pray   Write Things You Want to pray for.

I Love...

Sermon Title (or Subject)

_____

Date

_____

Today's Bible Verses

_____
_____
_____

Key Words

When you hear one of the words below...put a check by it.

- ☐ Land
- ☐ River
- ☐ Lord
- ☐ said
- ☐ Sacrifice
- ☐ Gift
- ☐ Worship
- ☐ Need
- ☐ Spirit
- ☐ Power
- ☐ Hope
- ☐ Joy
- ☐ Give
- ☐ Father
- ☐ Prophet

Notes:

Write your favorite things about today's sermon.

_____
_____
_____
_____
_____
_____
_____
_____
_____
_____

Draw a Picture of Today's Bible Story

My Favorite
Song From
Today is...

COUNT
How many times
the preacher
says the word
"Christian."

〣 I

Pray   Write Things You Want to pray for.

I Love...

Sermon Title (or Subject)

_____

Date

_____

Today's Bible Verses

_____
_____
_____

Key Words

When you hear one of the words below...put a check by it.

- [ ] Life
- [ ] Pray
- [ ] Obey
- [ ] Help
- [ ] Temple
- [ ] Idol
- [ ] Rose
- [ ] Grave
- [ ] Israel
- [ ] Holy
- [ ] Follow
- [ ] Study
- [ ] Word
- [ ] Amen
- [ ] Tempt

Notes:

Write your favorite things about today's sermon.

_____
_____
_____
_____
_____
_____
_____
_____
_____
_____

Draw a Picture of Today's Bible Story

My Favorite Song From Today is...

_____
_____
_____

Count
How many times the preacher says the word "Verse."

卌 I

Pray
Write Things You Want to pray for.

I Love...

Sermon Title (or Subject)

_____

Date

_____

Today's Bible Verses

_____
_____
_____

Key Words
When you hear one of the words below...put a check by it.

☐ Believe   ☐ Ark   ☐ Faith

☐ Night   ☐ Bless   ☐ Blood

☐ Child   ☐ Day   ☐ Comfort

☐ Eternal   ☐ Father   ☐ Darkness

☐ Gospel   ☐ Hope   ☐ Life

Notes:
Write your favorite things about today's sermon.

_____
_____
_____
_____
_____
_____
_____
_____
_____
_____

Draw a Picture of Today's Bible Story

My Favorite Song From Today is...

_____

_____

_____

Count
how many times the preacher says the word "You."

~~IIII~~ I

Pray
Write Things You want to pray for.

_____

_____

_____

_____

I Love...

Sermon Title (or Subject)

_____

Date

_____

Today's Bible Verses

_____

Key Words

When you hear one of the words below...put a check by it.

- ☐ Brother
- ☐ Lust
- ☐ Mercy
- ☐ Disciple
- ☐ Preach
- ☐ King
- ☐ Saint
- ☐ Church
- ☐ Thank
- ☐ Sin
- ☐ Trust
- ☐ Work
- ☐ Suffer
- ☐ Angel
- ☐ Victory

Notes:

Write your favorite things about today's sermon.

_____
_____
_____
_____
_____
_____
_____
_____
_____
_____
_____

Draw a Picture of Today's Bible Story

My Favorite Song From Today is...

Count
How many times the preacher says the word "Believe."

Pray   Write Things You want to pray for.

I Love...

Sermon Title (or Subject)

_____

Date

_____

Today's Bible Verses

_____
_____
_____

Key Words

When you hear one of the words below...put a check by it.

- ☐ Pray
- ☐ God
- ☐ Bible
- ☐ Good
- ☐ Jesus
- ☐ Glory
- ☐ Heaven
- ☐ Repent
- ☐ Lord
- ☐ Obey
- ☐ Fire
- ☐ Mercy
- ☐ Love
- ☐ Gospel
- ☐ Saved

Notes:

Write your favorite things about today's sermon.

_____
_____
_____
_____
_____
_____
_____
_____
_____
_____
_____

Draw a Picture of Today's Bible Story

My Favorite Song From Today is...

_____

_____

_____

Count
How many times the preacher says the word "Gospel."

Pray — Write Things You Want to pray for.

_____

_____

_____

_____

I Love...

Sermon Title (or Subject)

_____

Date
_____

Today's Bible Verses
_____
_____
_____

Key Words
When you hear one of the words below...put a check by it.

- ☐ Rejoice
- ☐ Serve
- ☐ Lord
- ☐ Cross
- ☐ Spirit
- ☐ Bread
- ☐ Worship
- ☐ Charity
- ☐ Spirit
- ☐ Evil
- ☐ Serve
- ☐ Joy
- ☐ Know
- ☐ Blessed
- ☐ Prophet

Notes:
Write your favorite things about today's sermon.

_____
_____
_____
_____
_____
_____
_____
_____
_____
_____
_____

✏️ Draw a Picture of Today's Bible Story

My Favorite Song From Today is...

_____

_____

_____

COUNT
How many times the preacher says the word "All."

𝍷𝍷𝍷𝍷𝍷 𝍷

Pray
Write Things You Want to pray for.

_____

_____

_____

_____

I Love...

Sermon Title (or Subject)

_____

Date

_____

Today's Bible Verses

_____
_____
_____

Key Words

When you hear one of the words below...put a check by it.

- ☐ Hope
- ☐ Pray
- ☐ Obey
- ☐ Able
- ☐ Sinner
- ☐ Christ
- ☐ Rose
- ☐ Grave
- ☐ Love
- ☐ Paul
- ☐ Say
- ☐ Study
- ☐ Word
- ☐ Amen
- ☐ King

Notes:

Write your favorite things about today's sermon.

_____
_____
_____
_____
_____
_____
_____
_____
_____
_____

Draw a Picture of Today's Bible Story

My Favorite Song From Today is...

Count
How many times the preacher says the word "Life."

Pray Write Things You Want to pray for.

I Love...

Sermon Title (or Subject)

_____

Date
_____

Today's Bible Verses

_____
_____
_____

Key Words
When you hear one of the words below...put a check by it.

- ☐ Pride
- ☐ Ark
- ☐ Believe
- ☐ Birth
- ☐ Child
- ☐ Blood
- ☐ Pure
- ☐ Church
- ☐ Comfort
- ☐ Wife
- ☐ Father
- ☐ Fruit
- ☐ Gospel
- ☐ Deacon
- ☐ Life

Notes:
Write your favorite things about today's sermon.

_____
_____
_____
_____
_____
_____
_____
_____
_____
_____

Draw a Picture of Today's Bible Story

My Favorite Song From Today is...

_____

_____

_____

Count

How many times the preacher says the word "We."

~~HHH~~ I

Pray

Write Things You Want to pray for.

_____

_____

_____

_____

I Love...

Sermon Title (or Subject)

_____

Date
_____

Today's Bible Verses
_____
_____
_____

Key Words
When you hear one of the words below...put a check by it.

- [ ] Husband
- [ ] Lust
- [ ] Mercy
- [ ] Grace
- [ ] Poor
- [ ] King
- [ ] All
- [ ] Give
- [ ] Thank
- [ ] Sin
- [ ] Trust
- [ ] Work
- [ ] Unity
- [ ] Wife
- [ ] Not

Notes:
Write your favorite things about today's sermon.

_____
_____
_____
_____
_____
_____
_____
_____
_____
_____

Draw a Picture of Today's Bible Story

My Favorite Song From Today is...

_____

_____

_____

Count
How many times the preacher says the word "Man."

~~HHH~~ I

Pray
Write Things You Want to pray for.

_____

_____

_____

_____

I Love...

Sermon Title (or Subject)

_____

Date

_____

Today's Bible Verses

_____
_____
_____

Key Words

When you hear one of the words below...put a check by it.

- [ ] Grace
- [ ] God
- [ ] Bible
- [ ] Jesus
- [ ] Faith
- [ ] Glory
- [ ] Heaven
- [ ] Repent
- [ ] Crucified
- [ ] Peace
- [ ] Trial
- [ ] Mercy
- [ ] Love
- [ ] Gospel
- [ ] Saved

Notes:

Write your favorite things about today's sermon.

_____
_____
_____
_____
_____
_____
_____
_____
_____
_____

Draw a Picture of Today's Bible Story

My Favorite Song From Today is...

_____

_____

_____

Count

How many times the preacher says the word "God."

~~HHH~~ I

Pray
Write Things You Want to Pray for.

_____

_____

_____

_____

I Love...

Sermon Title (or Subject)

_____

Date

_____

Today's Bible Verses

_____
_____
_____

Key Words

When you hear one of the words below...put a check by it.

- ☐ Holy
- ☐ Serve
- ☐ Lord
- ☐ Cross
- ☐ Sacrifice
- ☐ Gift
- ☐ Worship
- ☐ Charity
- ☐ Spirit
- ☐ Power
- ☐ Hope
- ☐ Joy
- ☐ Give
- ☐ Blessed
- ☐ Prophet

Notes:

Write your favorite things about today's sermon.

_____
_____
_____
_____
_____
_____
_____
_____
_____
_____

Draw a Picture of Today's Bible Story

My Favorite Song From Today is...

COUNT How many times the preacher says the word "Jesus."

卌 I

Pray   Write Things You Want to pray for.

I Love...

Sermon Title (or Subject)

_____

Date

_____

Today's Bible Verses

_____
_____
_____

Key Words

When you hear one of the words below...put a check by it.

- ☐ Altar
- ☐ Pray
- ☐ Obey
- ☐ Help
- ☐ Temple
- ☐ Christ
- ☐ Rose
- ☐ Grave
- ☐ Israel
- ☐ Baptize
- ☐ Sing
- ☐ Study
- ☐ Word
- ☐ Amen
- ☐ Scripture

Notes:

Write your favorite things about today's sermon.

_____
_____
_____
_____
_____
_____
_____
_____
_____
_____

Draw a Picture of Today's Bible Story

My Favorite Song From Today is...

_____

_____

_____

Count
How many times the preacher says the word "Lord."

~~卌~~ |

Pray
Write Things You Want to pray for.

_____

_____

_____

_____

I Love...

Sermon Title (or Subject)

_____

Date

_____

Today's Bible Verses

_____
_____
_____

Key Words

When you hear one of the words below...put a check by it.

- [ ] Apostle
- [ ] Ark
- [ ] Follow
- [ ] Birth
- [ ] Bless
- [ ] Blood
- [ ] Child
- [ ] Church
- [ ] Comfort
- [ ] Eternal
- [ ] Father
- [ ] Fruit
- [ ] Gospel
- [ ] Heart
- [ ] Life

Notes:

Write your favorite things about today's sermon.

_____
_____
_____
_____
_____
_____
_____
_____
_____
_____

Draw a Picture of Today's Bible Story

My Favorite Song From Today is...

_____

_____

_____

Count
How many times the preacher says the word "Spirit."

~~IIII~~ I

Pray
Write Things You want to pray for.

_____

_____

_____

_____

I Love...

Sermon Title (or Subject)

_____

Date

_____

Today's Bible Verses

_____
_____
_____

Key Words

When you hear one of the words below...put a check by it.

- [ ] Son
- [ ] Lust
- [ ] Mercy
- [ ] Grace
- [ ] Preach
- [ ] King
- [ ] Saint
- [ ] Sheep
- [ ] Thank
- [ ] Sin
- [ ] Trust
- [ ] Work
- [ ] Unity
- [ ] Study
- [ ] Victory

Notes:

Write your favorite things about today's sermon.

_____
_____
_____
_____
_____
_____
_____
_____
_____
_____
_____

Draw a Picture of Today's Bible Story

My Favorite Song From Today is...

Count

How many times the preacher says the word "Bible."

Pray   Write Things you want to pray for.

I Love...

Sermon Title (or Subject)

_____

Date

_____

Today's Bible Verses

_____
_____
_____

Key Words
When you hear one of the words below...put a check by it.

- [ ] Sea
- [ ] God
- [ ] Bible
- [ ] Mother
- [ ] Faith
- [ ] Glory
- [ ] Heaven
- [ ] Father
- [ ] Crucified
- [ ] Land
- [ ] Trial
- [ ] Jerusalem
- [ ] Love
- [ ] Gospel
- [ ] Saved

Notes:
Write your favorite things about today's sermon.

_____
_____
_____
_____
_____
_____
_____
_____
_____
_____

Draw a Picture of Today's Bible Story

My Favorite Song From Today is...

_____

_____

_____

COUNT how many times the preacher says the word "Family."

~~HHT~~ I

Pray Write Things You Want to pray for.

_____

_____

_____

_____

I Love...

Sermon Title (or Subject)

_____

Date

_____

Today's Bible Verses

_____
_____
_____

Key Words

When you hear one of the words below...put a check by it.

- ☐ Holy
- ☐ Serve
- ☐ Lord
- ☐ Moses
- ☐ Sacrifice
- ☐ Gift
- ☐ Worship
- ☐ Charity
- ☐ Testament
- ☐ Jewish
- ☐ Hope
- ☐ Joy
- ☐ Give
- ☐ Blessed
- ☐ Prophet

Notes:

Write your favorite things about today's sermon.

_____
_____
_____
_____
_____
_____
_____
_____
_____
_____
_____

✏️ Draw a Picture of Today's Bible Story

My Favorite Song From Today is...

_____

_____

_____

Count

How many times the preacher says the word "Live."

~~IIII~~ I

Pray   Write Things You Want to pray for.

_____

_____

_____

_____

I Love...

Sermon Title (or Subject)

_____

Date

_____

Today's Bible Verses

_____
_____
_____

Key Words

When you hear one of the words below...put a check by it.

- ☐ Change
- ☐ Bow
- ☐ Obey
- ☐ Help
- ☐ Temple
- ☐ Christ
- ☐ Flesh
- ☐ King
- ☐ Israel
- ☐ Baptize
- ☐ Sing
- ☐ Study
- ☐ World
- ☐ Amen
- ☐ Scripture

Notes:

Write your favorite things about today's sermon.

_____
_____
_____
_____
_____
_____
_____
_____
_____
_____
_____

Draw a Picture of Today's Bible Story

My Favorite Song From Today is...

_____

_____

_____

Count How many times the preacher says the word "New."

~~卌~~ |

Pray Write Things You Want to pray for.

_____
_____
_____
_____

I Love...

Sermon Title (or Subject)

_____

Date
_____

Today's Bible Verses
_____
_____
_____

Key Words
When you hear one of the words below...put a check by it.

- ☐ Paul
- ☐ Pride
- ☐ Believe
- ☐ Saved
- ☐ Bless
- ☐ Blood
- ☐ Child
- ☐ Church
- ☐ Boat
- ☐ Know
- ☐ Father
- ☐ Fruit
- ☐ Gospel
- ☐ Heart
- ☐ Life

Notes:
Write your favorite things about today's sermon.

_____
_____
_____
_____
_____
_____
_____
_____
_____
_____

Draw a Picture of Today's Bible Story

My Favorite Song From Today is...

Count
How many times the preacher says the word "Come."

Pray
Write Things you want to pray for.

I LOVE...

Sermon Title (or Subject)

_____

Date
_____

Today's Bible Verses

_____
_____
_____

Key Words

When you hear one of the words below...put a check by it.

- [ ] Help
- [ ] Way
- [ ] Mercy
- [ ] Listen
- [ ] Preach
- [ ] Love
- [ ] Saint
- [ ] Sheep
- [ ] Thank
- [ ] Good
- [ ] Trust
- [ ] Work
- [ ] Walk
- [ ] Study
- [ ] Victory

Notes:

Write your favorite things about today's sermon.

_____
_____
_____
_____
_____
_____
_____
_____
_____
_____
_____

Draw a Picture of Today's Bible Story

My Favorite Song From Today is...

_____

_____

_____

Count
How many times the preacher says the word "Heart."

~~HHH~~ |

Pray   Write Things you want to pray for.

I Love...

Sermon Title (or Subject)

_____

Date
_____

Today's Bible Verses
_____
_____
_____

Key Words
When you hear one of the words below...put a check by it.

- ☐ Ark
- ☐ God
- ☐ Bible

- ☐ Jesus
- ☐ Son
- ☐ Scripture

- ☐ Heaven
- ☐ Fruit
- ☐ Crucified

- ☐ Peace
- ☐ Trial
- ☐ Mercy

- ☐ Love
- ☐ Trust
- ☐ Saved

Notes:
Write your favorite things about today's sermon.

_____
_____
_____
_____
_____
_____
_____
_____
_____
_____

Draw a Picture of Today's Bible Story

My Favorite Song From Today is...

Count

How many times the preacher says the word "Life."

Pray   Write Things You Want to pray for.

I Love...

Sermon Title (or Subject)

_____

Date
_____

Today's Bible Verses
_____
_____
_____

Key Words
When you hear one of the words below...put a check by it.

- ☐ Amen
- ☐ Serve
- ☐ Mercy
- ☐ Cross
- ☐ Sacrifice
- ☐ Gift
- ☐ Worship
- ☐ Trust
- ☐ Spirit
- ☐ Work
- ☐ Hope
- ☐ Joy
- ☐ Give
- ☐ Blessed
- ☐ Unity

Notes:
Write your favorite things about today's sermon.

_____
_____
_____
_____
_____
_____
_____
_____
_____
_____
_____

Draw a Picture of Today's Bible Story

My Favorite Song From Today is…

Count
How many times the preacher says the word "Amen."

Pray — Write Things You Want to pray for.

I Love…

Sermon Title (or Subject)

_____

Date

_____

Today's Bible Verses

_____
_____
_____

Key Words
When you hear one of the words below...put a check by it.

- [ ] Altar
- [ ] Pray
- [ ] Obey
- [ ] Word
- [ ] Sin
- [ ] Saint
- [ ] Rose
- [ ] Grave
- [ ] Israel
- [ ] Heart
- [ ] Sing
- [ ] Study
- [ ] Blood
- [ ] Amen
- [ ] Scripture

Notes:
Write your favorite things about today's sermon.

_____
_____
_____
_____
_____
_____
_____
_____
_____
_____
_____

Draw a Picture of Today's Bible Story

My Favorite Song From Today is...

Count
How many times the preacher says the word "Sin."

HHH I

Pray
Write Things You Want to pray for.

I Love...

Sermon Title (or Subject)

_____

Date

_____

Today's Bible Verses

_____
_____
_____

Key Words

When you hear one of the words below...put a check by it.

- ☐ Grace
- ☐ Ark
- ☐ Believe
- ☐ Birth
- ☐ Lust
- ☐ Blood
- ☐ Sheep
- ☐ Church
- ☐ Preach
- ☐ Eternal
- ☐ Father
- ☐ Fruit
- ☐ Gospel
- ☐ Jesus
- ☐ Life

Notes:

Write your favorite things about today's sermon.

_____
_____
_____
_____
_____
_____
_____
_____
_____
_____

✏️ Draw a Picture of Today's Bible Story

My Favorite Song From Today is...

_____

_____

_____

Count

How many times the preacher says the word "Grace."

~~IIII~~ I

Pray Write Things You Want to pray for.

_____

_____

_____

_____

I Love...

Sermon Title (or Subject)

_____

Date

_____

Today's Bible Verses

_____
_____
_____

Key Words
When you hear one of the words below...put a check by it.

☐ Repent   ☐ Lust   ☐ Mercy

☐ Grace   ☐ God   ☐ Crucify

☐ Saint   ☐ Sheep   ☐ Thank

☐ Sin   ☐ Trust   ☐ Love

☐ Saved   ☐ Study   ☐ Victory

Notes:
Write your favorite things about today's sermon.

Draw a Picture of Today's Bible Story

My Favorite Song From Today is...

_____

_____

_____

Count

How many times the preacher says the word "Cross."

~~HHHH~~ I

Pray
Write Things you want to pray for.

_____

_____

_____

_____

I Love...

Sermon Title (or Subject)

_____

Date

_____

Today's Bible Verses

_____
_____
_____

Key Words

When you hear one of the words below...put a check by it.

☐ Holy   ☐ God   ☐ Bible

☐ Gift   ☐ Book   ☐ Glory

☐ Heaven   ☐ Repent   ☐ Crucified

☐ Joy   ☐ Author   ☐ Mercy

☐ Love   ☐ Gospel   ☐ Pray

Notes:

Write your favorite things about today's sermon.

_____
_____
_____
_____
_____
_____
_____
_____
_____
_____

Draw a Picture of Today's Bible Story

My Favorite Song From Today is...

_____

_____

_____

Count
How many times the preacher says the word "Look."

~~HHH~~ I

Pray   Write Things You Want to pray for.

_____

_____

_____

_____

I Love...

Sermon Title (or Subject)

_____

Date

_____

Today's Bible Verses

_____
_____
_____

Key Words

When you hear one of the words below...put a check by it.

- ☐ Spirit
- ☐ Serve
- ☐ Lord
- ☐ Cross
- ☐ Peace
- ☐ Gift
- ☐ Love
- ☐ Charity
- ☐ Page
- ☐ King
- ☐ Hope
- ☐ Joy
- ☐ Give
- ☐ Vision
- ☐ Blind

Notes:

Write your favorite things about today's sermon.

_____
_____
_____
_____
_____
_____
_____
_____
_____
_____

Draw a Picture of Today's Bible Story

My Favorite Song From Today is...

Count How many times the preacher says the word "Listen."

Ⅲ

Pray Write things you want to pray for.

I Love...

Sermon Title (or Subject)

_____

Date

_____

Today's Bible Verses

_____
_____
_____

Key Words
When you hear one of the words below...put a check by it.

- ☐ Lamb
- ☐ Pray
- ☐ Obey
- ☐ Help
- ☐ Thank
- ☐ Christ
- ☐ Comfort
- ☐ Grave
- ☐ Bless
- ☐ Blood
- ☐ Sing
- ☐ Garden
- ☐ Word
- ☐ Gift
- ☐ Scripture

Notes:
Write your favorite things about today's sermon.

_____
_____
_____
_____
_____
_____
_____
_____
_____
_____

Draw a Picture of Today's Bible Story

My Favorite Song From Today is...

_____

_____

_____

Count

How many times the preacher says the word "Gospel."

~~HHH~~ I

Pray

Write Things you want to pray for.

_____

_____

_____

_____

I Love...

Sermon Title (or Subject)

_____

Date
_____

Today's Bible Verses
_____
_____
_____

Key Words
When you hear one of the words below...put a check by it.

- ☐ Grave
- ☐ Ark
- ☐ Israel
- ☐ Birth
- ☐ Sing
- ☐ Blood
- ☐ Study
- ☐ Church
- ☐ Comfort
- ☐ Child
- ☐ Father
- ☐ Virgin
- ☐ Gospel
- ☐ Heart
- ☐ Life

Notes:
Write your favorite things about today's sermon.

_____
_____
_____
_____
_____
_____
_____
_____
_____
_____

Draw a Picture of Today's Bible Story

My Favorite Song From Today is...

_____

_____

_____

Count
How many times the preacher says the word "him."

Pray — Write Things You Want to Pray for.

_____

_____

_____

_____

I Love...

Sermon Title (or Subject)

_____

Date

_____

Today's Bible Verses

_____
_____
_____

Key Words
When you hear one of the words below...put a check by it.

- ☐ Peter
- ☐ Lust
- ☐ Mercy
- ☐ Power
- ☐ Preach
- ☐ King
- ☐ Saint
- ☐ Sheep
- ☐ Pure
- ☐ Bible
- ☐ Trust
- ☐ Work
- ☐ Follow
- ☐ Study
- ☐ Trust

Notes:
Write your favorite things about today's sermon.

_____
_____
_____
_____
_____
_____
_____
_____
_____
_____

Draw a Picture of Today's Bible Story

My Favorite Song From Today is...

Count
How many times the preacher says the word "Church."

Pray Write Things You Want to Pray for.

I Love...

Sermon Title (or Subject)

_____

Date
_____

Today's Bible Verses

_____
_____
_____

Key Words
When you hear one of the words below...put a check by it.

- ☐ Prince
- ☐ Woman
- ☐ Bible
- ☐ Book
- ☐ Faith
- ☐ Glory
- ☐ Heaven
- ☐ Faith
- ☐ Crucified
- ☐ Egypt
- ☐ Trial
- ☐ Mercy
- ☐ Love
- ☐ Death
- ☐ Saved

Notes:
Write your favorite things about today's sermon.

_____
_____
_____
_____
_____
_____
_____
_____
_____
_____

Draw a Picture of Today's Bible Story

My Favorite Song From Today is...

_____

_____

_____

COUNT

How many times the preacher says the word "we."

~~HHH~~ 1

Pray   Write things you want to pray for.

_____

_____

_____

_____

I Love...

Sermon Title (or Subject)

_____

Date

_____

Today's Bible Verses

_____
_____
_____

Key Words

When you hear one of the words below...put a check by it.

- ☐ Land
- ☐ River
- ☐ Lord
- ☐ said
- ☐ Sacrifice
- ☐ Gift
- ☐ Worship
- ☐ Need
- ☐ Spirit
- ☐ Power
- ☐ Hope
- ☐ Joy
- ☐ Give
- ☐ Father
- ☐ Prophet

Notes:
Write your favorite things about today's sermon.

_____
_____
_____
_____
_____
_____
_____
_____
_____
_____

Draw a Picture of Today's Bible Story

My Favorite Song From Today is...

_____

_____

_____

Count How many times the preacher says the word "Christian."

卌 l

Pray Write Things You Want to pray for.

_____

_____

_____

_____

I Love...

Made in the USA
San Bernardino, CA
20 March 2017